The Dressing-up Book

Jane Bull

DK

LONDON, NEW YORK, MUNICH,
MELBOURNE, and DELHI

DESIGN • Jane Bull
EDITOR • Penelope Arlon
PHOTOGRAPHY • Andy Crawford
DESIGN ASSISTANT • Gemma Fletcher

PUBLISHING MANAGER • Sue Leonard
PRODUCTION • Angela Graef
DTP DESIGNER • Almudena Díaz

For **Charlotte, Billy, and James**

First American Edition, 2006
Published in the United States by
DK Publishing, Inc.
375 Hudson Street
New York, New York 10014

06 07 08 09 10   10 9 8 7 6 5 4 3 2 1

A Cataloging-in-Publication record for this
book is available from the Library of Congress.

ISBN 13: 978-0-7566-1983-1

ISBN 10: 0-7566-1983-1

Color reproduction by
GRB Editrice S.r.l., Verona, Italy
Printed and bound by Toppan, China

Discover more at
www.dk.com

I'm off to find that treasure!

A book full of characters...

become a trash bot...

...or star on TV!

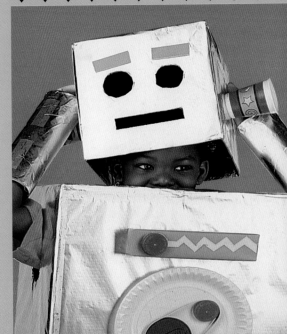

Let's dress up!

what's in the dress-up box?

Mom's shoes, Dad's shirt,
Grandma's handbag,
Auntie's beads?

Beads

Boots and shoes

Clothes

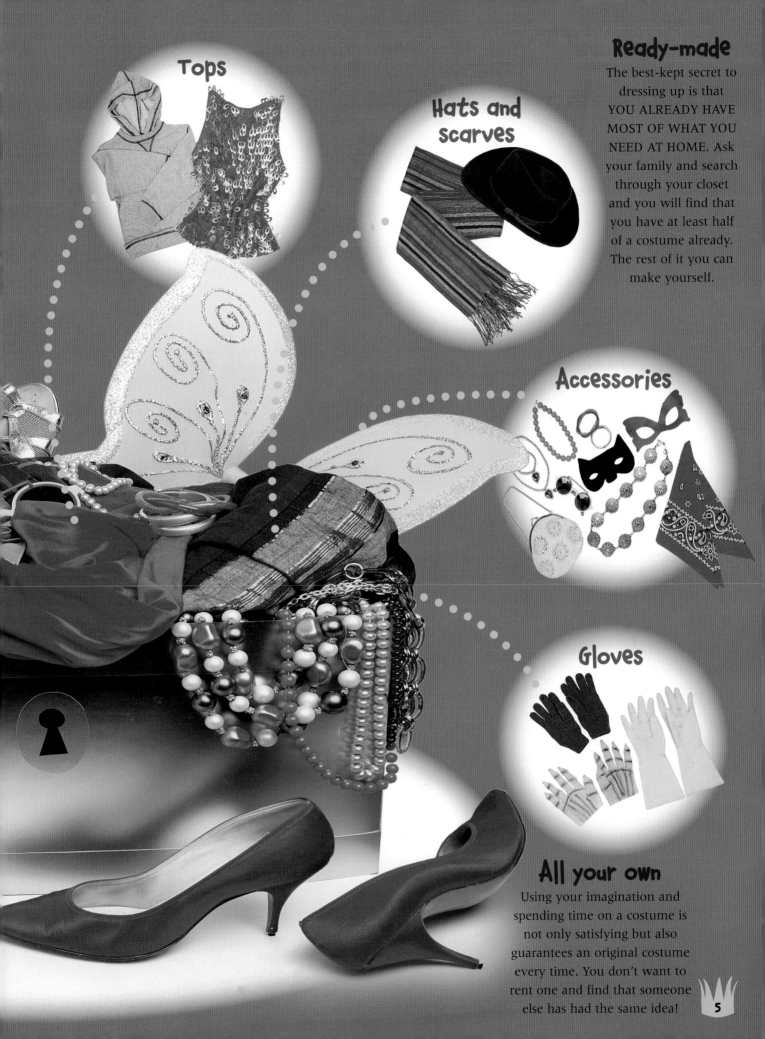

Tops

Hats and scarves

Accessories

Gloves

Ready-made

The best-kept secret to dressing up is that YOU ALREADY HAVE MOST OF WHAT YOU NEED AT HOME. Ask your family and search through your closet and you will find that you have at least half of a costume already. The rest of it you can make yourself.

All your own

Using your imagination and spending time on a costume is not only satisfying but also guarantees an original costume every time. You don't want to rent one and find that someone else has had the same idea!

5

Beads and boas

Look out Mom! We're after your frills and feathers for our own fashion parade.

On the catwalk

Most moms have a secret stash of beads and bangles that they haven't used in years. Get your friends to ask their moms too and hold a fashion show.

Bags of beads

Little angel

This little angel has homemade wings. Find out how to make them yourself on page 44.

Cool sunglasses

And the winner is...

Your catwalk wouldn't be complete without music and a microphone—make your own on page 48.

Feathers

For instant glamour, who can resist fancy, feathery boas.

Mom's dress

Wear it over your T-shirt.

Mom's top

It doubles as a dress!

Pile on the beads, swish around with a boa, and teeter along in high heels.

Use a red towel as a cape.

Be your own hero

An alien, a pirate, a witch, or Super-Boy—raid your closet and you'll be surprised what you can create with a little imagination.

What makes a pirate? A striped T-shirt and rolled-up pants.

Witch

What makes a witch? Striped tights!

Imp

See how to make my wings on page 44.

Turn to page 42 to find out how to make a witch's cape.

Jump-rope lasso

Yee ha! cowboy

A checked shirt, a jump-rope lasso, and a bandana are the basics for a Wild West cowboy costume.

Mini pirate

He's found the treasure!

Alien

Paint a face onto a balloon and put it inside a hooded sweatshirt. A very tall alien—it's out of this world!

Yellow rubber gloves

Super-Boy

Black tights, red socks, and a red towel as a cape. Save the world Super-Boy!

Safety pin the cape to your T-shirt.

You will need:

A mop, three sticks, masking tape, string, a stapler, a large shirt, and odds and ends to make the body.

Tape a small stick to the top of the mop for the shoulders.

Ask your Dad for an old shirt.

The hand sticks need to be the same length as the mop.

Gentle giant

Hello down there! Walk tall with the amazing smiling, waving giant. Find yourself a mop, a huge shirt, and two good friends to help him wave.

Decorate the face using a toilet-paper-roll nose and construction paper.

Drape the shirt over the shoulders, leaving a button undone for the mop holder to see out of.

Giant head

Cut a face shape out of cardboard and decorate it. Don't worry about the hair—the mop does the trick! Tape the face under the mop.

Make sure the face is positioned so that the mop hair falls stylishly.

Gently move the hand sticks from side to side and your giant will wave goodbye.

Hello, I'm up here!

I'm in here!
Put one of your friends inside the large shirt to hold the mop, and the other two will hold the hands.

Tie a piece of string around the hand and tape the string ends to the stick.

Giant hands
Draw around your hands, but twice the size, on a piece of cardboard, and cut out. Tie a piece of string around the stick, then around the hand.

Staple the shirt sleeves to the hand.

Practice together to give your giant the best moves.

welcome to Box TV!
I'm Katie Kardboard—here's the news.

Box mania is sweeping the country. Everyone is going box crazy! Our reporter Cody Carton is in the field. What can you tell us Cody?

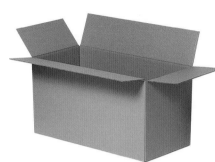

Box TV

Make a Box TV

To become newscaster Katie Kardboard, cut a square hole in the side of a box. Glue a strip of foil around the edge and some bottle tops along the bottom as knobs. Now climb inside and get reporting.

For the antenna, bend a wire coat hanger in half...

...and tape it to the top of the box.

Yes, that's right Katie, it's raining boxes out here! All over the country cardboard boxes are being magically transformed into awesome outfits. Check out these gallant knights and fairy princesses on horseback, Wild West rodeo cowboys, and recycled robots. Viewers—it's all the rage so get wrapping! And that just about wraps it up for me too.

This is Cody Carton for Box TV— back to the studio

Find out how to make the microphone on page 48.

13

The big box cover-up

The first step toward getting boxed up is to find a box as big as you! When you have found it you need to learn how to wrap it up.

Choose your box

Find the biggest box you can. Decide which is the top, bottom, and sides, and cut the flaps off or tape them down.

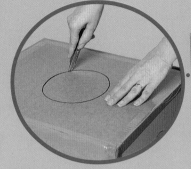

Cut out holes for your arms and head.

Ask an adult: to help you cut out the holes and get your box ready.

Cover-up materials

Large pieces of paper, rolls of gift wrapping paper, aluminum foil, and Kraft paper are all perfect for wrapping boxes.

How to cover up

1 Lay your box on the rolled-out paper, wrap it around the box, and trim the end.

Turn the box on its side.

Trim the paper so it fits around the corner of the box.

Fold the paper inside the edge of the box and tape it in place.

2 Flatten the paper down the sides of the box.

3 Tape the paper down, ignoring the holes at this stage.

4 Cut pieces of paper to cover the sides of the box and tape in position.

Turn the box on its side.

Holes for head and arms

Find the holes and carefully cut slits in the paper. Fold them inside and tape.

Ask an adult: to help cut out the holes.

Tape the paper in position.

Now turn the page to decorate.

All wrapped up!

15

walking presents

Very special delivery—wrap yourself up as an enormous present and deliver yourself to the party!

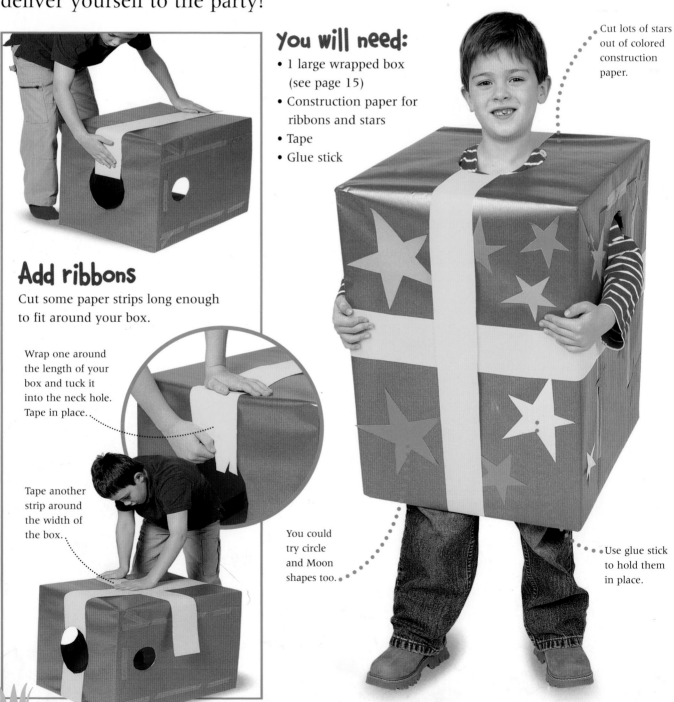

You will need:
- 1 large wrapped box (see page 15)
- Construction paper for ribbons and stars
- Tape
- Glue stick

Cut lots of stars out of colored construction paper.

Add ribbons
Cut some paper strips long enough to fit around your box.

Wrap one around the length of your box and tuck it into the neck hole. Tape in place.

Tape another strip around the width of the box.

You could try circle and Moon shapes too.

Use glue stick to hold them in place.

Mega box

If you find a really big box, try making the hole at the front for your face to peep through.

Hello down there!

If you use festive wrapping paper, there is no need to add extra decorations.

Make a paper bow to attach to a headband.

These snazzy socks match this polka-dot box. Find some of your own and match your box too.

Recycled robots

You will need:

Cardboard boxes—
   big and small
Cardboard tubes
Aluminum foil
Paper plates
Double-sided tape

" **My name is Box-bot** and if you follow my instructions I can help you re-create me."

Building Box-bot

All you need for this brilliant bot is lots of boxes—big and small—and cartons, paper plates, and anything else that can be recycled. Silver-painted knee-pads, shoe-box shoes, and rubber gloves finish him off.

Ask an adult:
to help cut out the holes.

Cut out the robot face.

Head box

Cardboard tubes for arms.

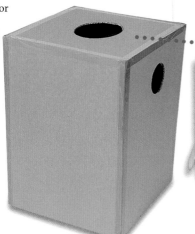

Body box

These are the pads you use with your in-line skates.

Knee pads

Cut a hole to put your foot through.

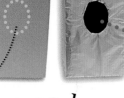

Shoe box

Glue on paper cups for ears.

Add some cardboard tubes to look like controls.

Catch you later, fairy friends!

Giddy-up horsey

Get on your horse and into battle or a cowboy

yeee haa!

whoa, steady boy!

Horse themes

There are so many different horse themes you could try, such as Black Beauty with a white star on its forehead or a mythical Pegasus with wings.

ride! Become a knight on your trusted steed galloping on the range, and is there a fairy horse here, too?

Start collecting your horse boxes

Horse boxes

Find a large box and turn it on its side. It needs to be big enough for you to fit inside and for your pretend legs to hang over the side.

Make your galloping horses

Follow these steps and you'll end up with a basic horse shape. You can then decorate it how you like or turn the pages for some wild ideas.

Horse body

Find a cardboard box that's big enough for you to fit inside.

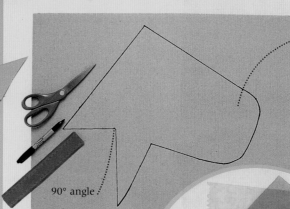

Cut off the long flaps at the top and all the bottom flaps.

Use strong packing tape to secure the short flaps.

Cut out some colored paper and glue it to each end first.

Fold the paper over neatly and tape in place.

Measure the paper against the box and cut it to size.

You could snip the bottom edge of the paper into a pattern.

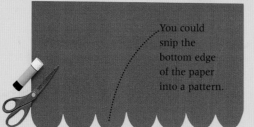

When you have taped the ends down, glue the sides in place.

Horse head

Draw a simple horse's head shape onto a piece of cardboard.

Cut out the shape, then trace both sides onto construction paper (see bottom).

90° angle

Tape the head in place on the box.

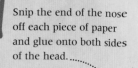

To hide the tape, glue strips of paper over it.

Snip the end of the nose off each piece of paper and glue onto both sides of the head.

As a guide, lay the cardboard shape on the construction paper and draw around it. Turn it over and draw it again. Cut out both shapes.

Ask an adult to help with the box cutting.

You will need:

Large cardboard box • construction paper to cover horse • cardboard for head • scissors • pens • ribbons • glue • tape

Reins

For sturdy reins to control your wild horse, thread some ribbon through the nose.

To add a noseband, cut a strip of paper and glue it along the nose line.

Ask an adult: to help make the hole.

Use the point of a pen to make a hole big enough to thread some ribbon through for reins.

Tail

Make a tail out of a piece of paper the same color as the horse.

Cut out a large square piece of paper to the length you want for the tail.

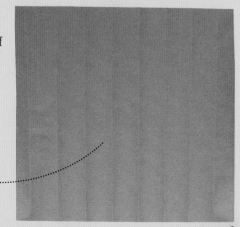

Fold the paper over and over and cut it into strips, leaving the top uncut.

Stick the tail onto the horse with tape.

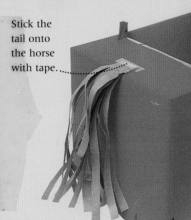

Shoulder straps

Use ribbon for the straps. Attach them to the box and adjust the length so your horse hangs at the right height.

Make four holes with the point of a pen.

Ask an adult: to help make the holes.

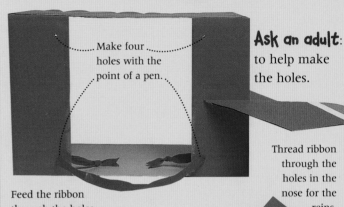

Feed the ribbon through the holes and tie a knot in each end.

Thread ribbon through the holes in the nose for the reins.

If the straps are too long tie the knot farther up to make the strap shorter.

Now let's show them how to decorate you

Tip If the straps slip off your shoulders, tape them together at the back.

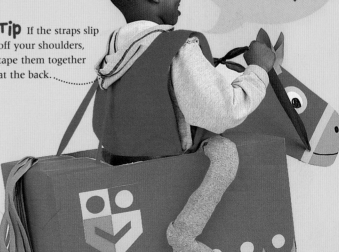

Horsey types

How many are there? About as many as your imagination can stretch to. Magical beasts like a unicorn and a Pegasus can be all kinds of colors, while cowboys might prefer a more natural horse color.

Fake legs

Take a pair of long socks and stuff them with aluminum foil (this makes them easy to shape). Tape them to the box as shown and glue the foot to the side.

Use strong glue on the socks.

Tape the leg to the inside of the box.

Ears

Cut two ear shapes out of paper, fold them over at the base, and glue together. Attach to the head using double-sided tape.

Use the shoulder straps to carry your horse.

Choose some suitable pants or tights to wear underneath the horse.

24

Fake legs made from pants

Cowboy's legs

Instead of stuffed socks for legs, try draping a pair of pants across the horse, then stuffing the leg end into some shoes.

Magical Unicorn

A unicorn needs a horn. This one is made of cardboard and covered in gold paper and ribbon. Gather together all your sparkly odds and ends for this special horse.

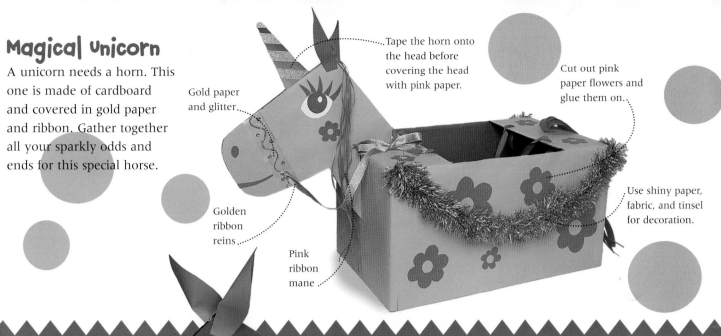

Gold paper and glitter

Golden ribbon reins

Pink ribbon mane

Tape the horn onto the head before covering the head with pink paper.

Cut out pink paper flowers and glue them on.

Use shiny paper, fabric, and tinsel for decoration.

Knight rider

Regal reds and heraldic shields.

Make an eye with white paper glued to a yellow oval shape.

Mark on the nose, eye, and mouth with felt pen.

Yellow paper spots help to make a regal cape.

Make a heraldic shield from colored paper.

Prairie boy

A palomino pony with brown paper patches.

Mark on the nose and mouth with felt pen.

Red paper strips make the bridle straps.

Cut out blob shapes from brown paper and stick them on with glue.

Cut out a saddle shape from black paper.

A knight in shining armor

A true knight needs full armor and weapons. A simple tunic, a shield, a helmet, and a sword are perfect for a shining knight.

Cardboard tube sword
Use the tube from a roll of wrapping paper. A small tube makes a good dagger.

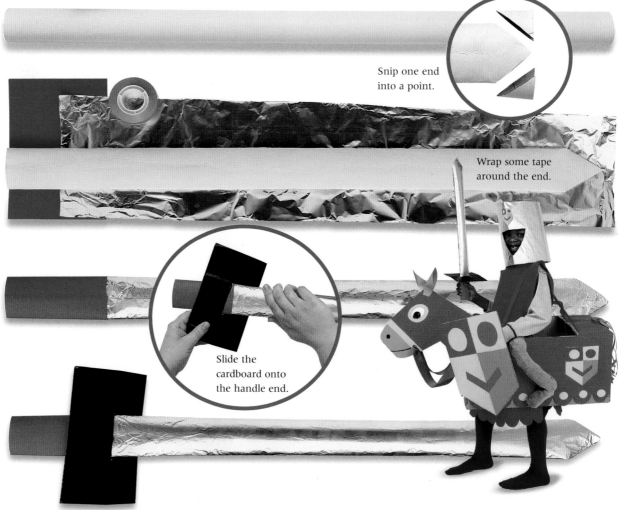

Take a long tube and squash it flat.

Snip one end into a point.

Cover the sword with aluminum foil, then tape a strip of red paper around the handle end.

Wrap some tape around the end.

Cut out a small rectangle of cardboard, paint it black, and cut a slit through the center.

Slide the cardboard onto the handle end.

The perfect, shining sword.

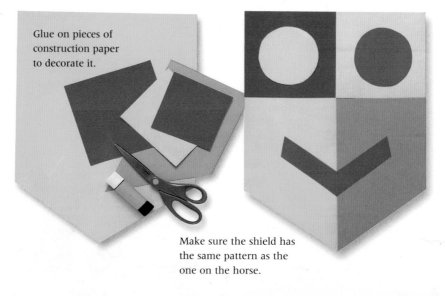

Shield
Choose your design carefully for your shield—it will show your family crest.

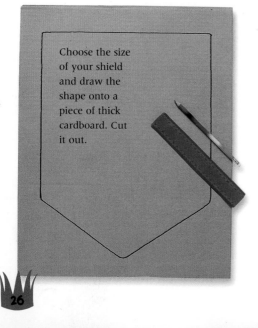

Choose the size of your shield and draw the shape onto a piece of thick cardboard. Cut it out.

Glue on pieces of construction paper to decorate it.

Make sure the shield has the same pattern as the one on the horse.

26

Tunic

The idea for this is simple—take a long piece of material, fold it in half, cut a slash along the fold for your head to go through, and tie it around the waist with a belt.

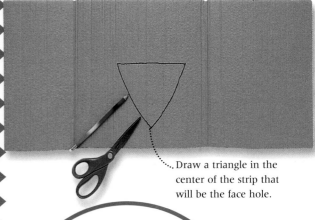

Belt

Cut a slit along the fold—big enough to fit your head through.

Gray wool gloves

Knight's outfit

To create the right look, wear a hooded top under your tunic—good for the chain-mail effect. Long gray socks and gloves also go well with the outfit. Now pick up your shield, helmet, and sword and become the knight in shining armor.

Make a handle.

Stick a strip of cardboard to the back of a shield as a handle for you to hold it with.

Long gray socks

Helmet

Cut a strip of cardboard long enough to wrap around your head, and taller than the distance from your shoulder to the top of your head.

Draw a triangle in the center of the strip that will be the face hole.

Cut the face hole out, making sure it is in the right place, and tape the helmet's ends together.

Turn the helmet upside-down and draw around it on cardboard.

Cut the shape out.

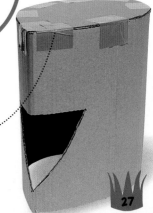

Tape the lid onto the helmet, cover it in aluminum foil, and decorate with your crest.

27

Pirates on the high seas

Ha harr me hearties jump aboard,
we're off to find the treasure!

You could make a saber similar to the knight's sword on page 26.

Sea legs
Wear blue tights to look like the sea.

Ship ahoy!
A cardboard box pirate ship, a Jolly Roger flag, and a lethal saber together with a bag of provisions, and you are ready to sail the high seas to find the hidden treasure!

Mmm...
good treasure, lucky I found it!

Anchors aweigh!

Find a piece of thick cardboard for your ship's anchor.

Draw the shape

Draw an anchor shape and cut it out.

Wrap in foil

Fold the foil around the cardboard, shape it, and tape it.

Hang it on your boat

Tie some string through the hole and tape it to your boat.

Find me some jewels

Treasure chest

Make a treasure chest to complete your pirate look. Find a box with a lid, decorate it with paper, and fill it up with all your jewels and silver coins.

Tape a piece of cardboard to a stick for a Jolly Roger flag.

Land ahoy!

How to make your boat

Follow the steps to show you how to make a boat. But remember, it doesn't have to end up as a pirate ship, you could add speedy white stripes for a fast power boat.

Boat shape

Try to find a cardboard box that you can fit inside—you also want it to be fairly long.

Cut off the long flaps from the top and all the flaps off the bottom.

Use packing tape to secure the small flaps.

Cut out a piece of cardboard that will curve onto the front of the boat.

Make sure it is taped securely.

Tape it to both sides.

Cut a piece of cardboard to fit on the top.

Tape it into place.

Cover the boat

Now you have your boat shape, it's time to wrap it. Use colored paper—construction or Kraft paper work well.

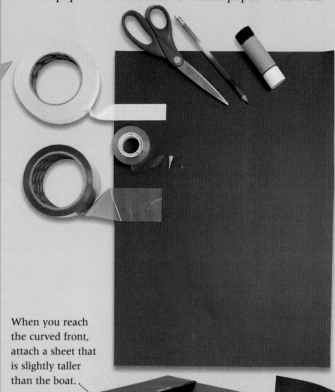

When you reach the curved front, attach a sheet that is slightly taller than the boat.

Snip the overhang down to the top of the boat all along, as shown.

Lay each bit flat and tape in place.

Finally, cut a piece of paper to fit on the top at the front and glue it in place—this hides the messy ends.

Ask an adult
to help cut the cardboard.

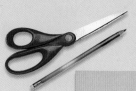

Add decorations
Now for the fun part—the decoration!

Cut some portholes out of colored paper.

You will also need strips of paper to line the top of the boat.

Anchor shapes are good for decoration too.

Glue a band of waves onto the bottom of your boat.

Draw a wave shape on blue paper and cut it out.

Shoulder straps
Once the shoulder straps are on, you are set to sail.

Climb into the box and hold it where it is comfortable.

Ask an adult:
to help with this part.

See page 23 to find out how to attach the shoulder straps.

Now you are ready for the high seas!

Car body

You will need a cardboard box, large enough for you to fit inside.

Cut all the flaps off the bottom of the box.

Cut the long flaps off the top.

Tape the short ends down.

Wrap the box up with colored paper.

See page 22 for wrapping tips.

Car parts

Collect up some odds and ends for decoration.

Paper cup

Paper bowls or plates

Cardboard tubes and boxes

Driving in my car

Attach some straps—follow the steps on page 23.

Paper-plate steering wheel.

Paint black lines for the doors.

I like driving in my cardboard car. It gets me here, there, and everywhere!

beep beep!

Car parts

You will need paper plates, paper cups, aluminum foil, and some construction paper to make your car parts.

Headlights and grill

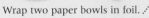

Wrap two paper bowls in foil.

Paper bowl

Glue two paper circles inside.

Wrap a box in foil and add black stripes for the grill. Stick them on with double-sided tape.

Bumpers

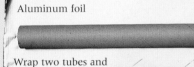

Aluminum foil

Cardboard tube from inside the foil.

Wrap two tubes and tuck in the ends.

Rear lights

Paper cup

Glue some red construction paper inside.

Cut two cups in half.

Wrap them in foil.

Use double-sided tape to attach the decorations to the car.

Wheels

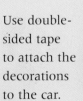

Paper bowl or plate

Glue two circles of paper to the plate.

Paint on the tires.

... A box wrapped in yellow paper makes a good trunk.

Along the roads ...

beep beep!

around the bends ...

I then ...

... stop off to see my friends.

Fairy princess

with a wave of the wand
become a princess from head to toe.

A fairy outfit

To create the fairy look you need a paper crown, a pink T-shirt tucked into a paper skirt, and fancy slippers. Finish with bangles and beads and, of course, a cape (see page 43).

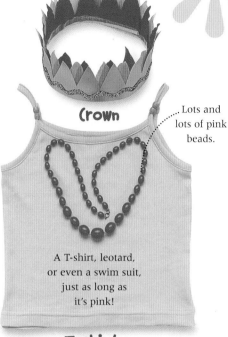

Crown

Lots and lots of pink beads.

A T-shirt, leotard, or even a swim suit, just as long as it's pink!

T-shirt

Crepe-paper skirt

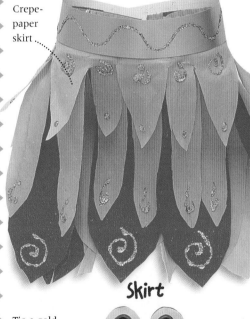

Skirt

Tie a gold bow to your shoes to add some fairy sparkle.

Shoes

A magic wand

Cut out two gold stars. Tape one to the end of a long stick then glue the other on top. Decorate the stick with a ribbon.

35

How to make a fancy fairy

Crepe paper is great to use—it's tough but flimsy like fabric. You don't just have to make a pink one—try a green and purple one for a Halloween fairy.

Waistband

Cut a piece of gold cardboard about 2 in (5 cm) wide and long enough to fit around your waist, with 6 in (15 cm) extra to fasten it.

Crepe-paper skirt

Cut out sheet of crepe paper wide enough to fit around your waist with an overlap, and long enough to reach your knees.

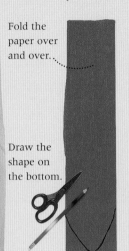

Fold the paper over and over.

Cut along the fold lines, but not all the way to the top.

Draw the shape on the bottom.

Snip around the shape.

Fairy crown

You can't be a real fairy without a fairy crown! Use your leftover gold cardboard and crepe paper to conjure a crown fit for a fairy princess.

Tape the ends of the cardboard to make the crown shape.

Cut the strips about 2 in (5 cm) wide and long enough to fit around your head, with a little extra for fastening.

1 Cut a strip of gold cardboard and two pieces of crepe paper.

Cut cardboard and paper into points.

Tape the crepe paper to the cardboard back.

2 Tape the paper strips to the back of the cardboard.

First apply the glue, then sprinkle the glitter.

Glitter

Glue

3 Decorate with glitter and leave to dry before taping the ends together.

Now do the same with
another piece of crepe
paper—try different lengths.

Unfold
the paper.

Keep taping on
layers of paper.

Tape the paper
to the back
of the gold
cardboard.

With craft glue, squeeze
some shapes on the
front of your skirt.

Pink magic

Finish your fairy outfit by adding pink
accessories. Search around your house—
you may find some pink beads and
bangles to wear. Turn to page 43 to find
out how to make the fairy cape.

Sprinkle glitter
on the glue and
let it dry.

Fasten your skirt
with Velcro.

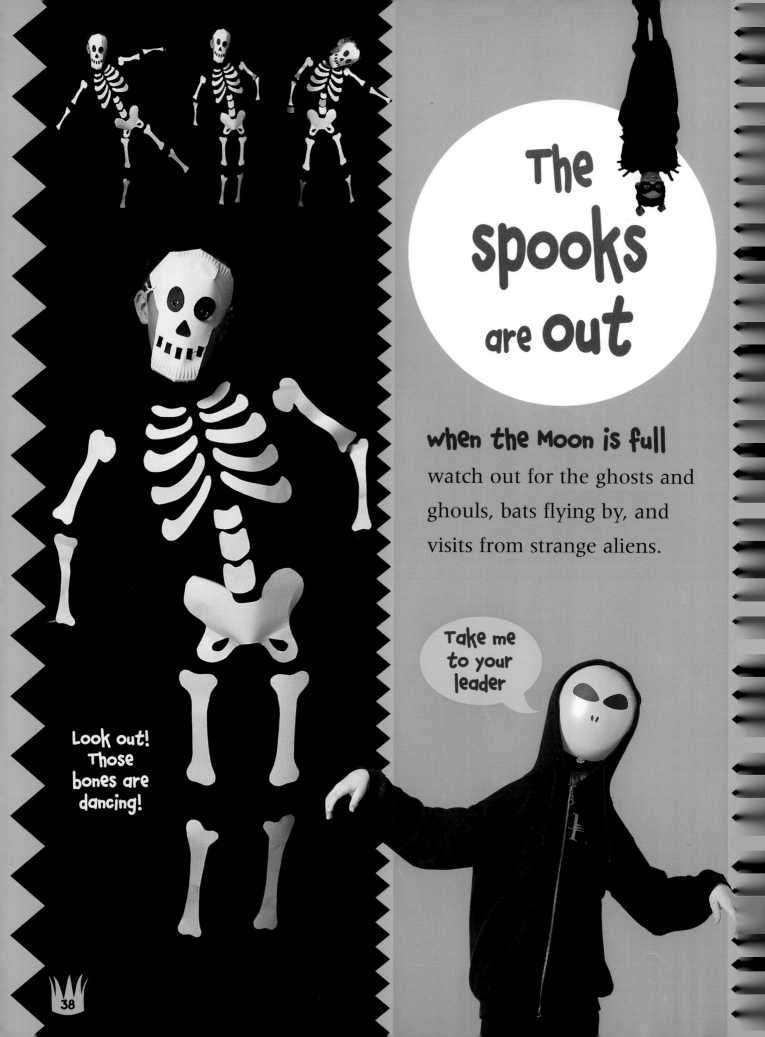

The spooks are out

when the Moon is full watch out for the ghosts and ghouls, bats flying by, and visits from strange aliens.

Look out! Those bones are dancing!

Take me to your leader

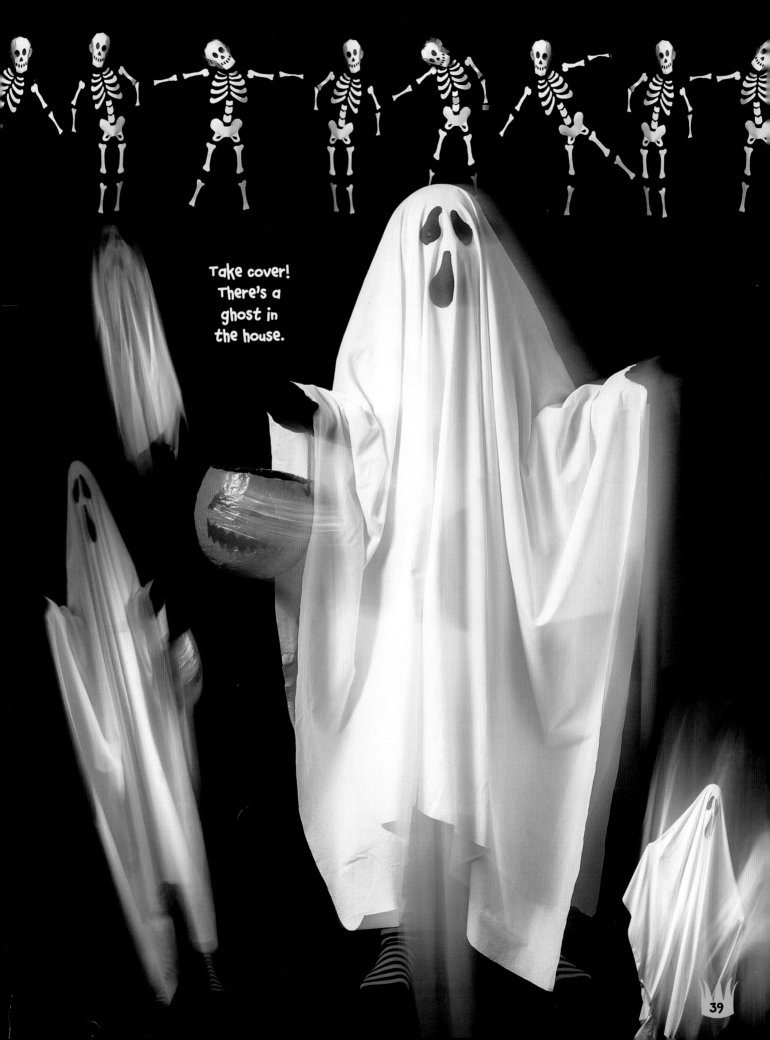

Take cover!
There's a
ghost in
the house.

Screaming spooks

Send shivers down spines at the witching hour by becoming this spooky specter.

Ask your mom if she has a spare white sheet.

Draw some spooky eyes and a mouth shape out of black felt and cut them out.

Creepy costume

The spooky ghost is a great costume for a Halloween party, but you may have to take it off when you want to eat or talk, so make sure you wear party clothes underneath.

Glue the eyes and mouth onto the sheet with craft glue and cut tiny holes in the eyes so you can see.

Try the sheet on for size. You may have to cut it— you don't want to trip on it.

Skull mask

A good skeleton needs a skull mask.

Take a paper plate and draw these outlines on it.

Cut along these lines.

Overlap the flap where you have made the slits at the top.

Glue in place on both sides.

Draw holes where your eyes will go and cut them out.

Cut eyes, a nose, and teeth out of construction paper.

Make a hole on each side of the face and thread some elastic through to tie it around your head.

Knot

Put the features on with glue.

Wear your mask with your funny-bones outfit.

Funny bones

No one will be laughing at these funny bones—they'll be shaking in their shoes!

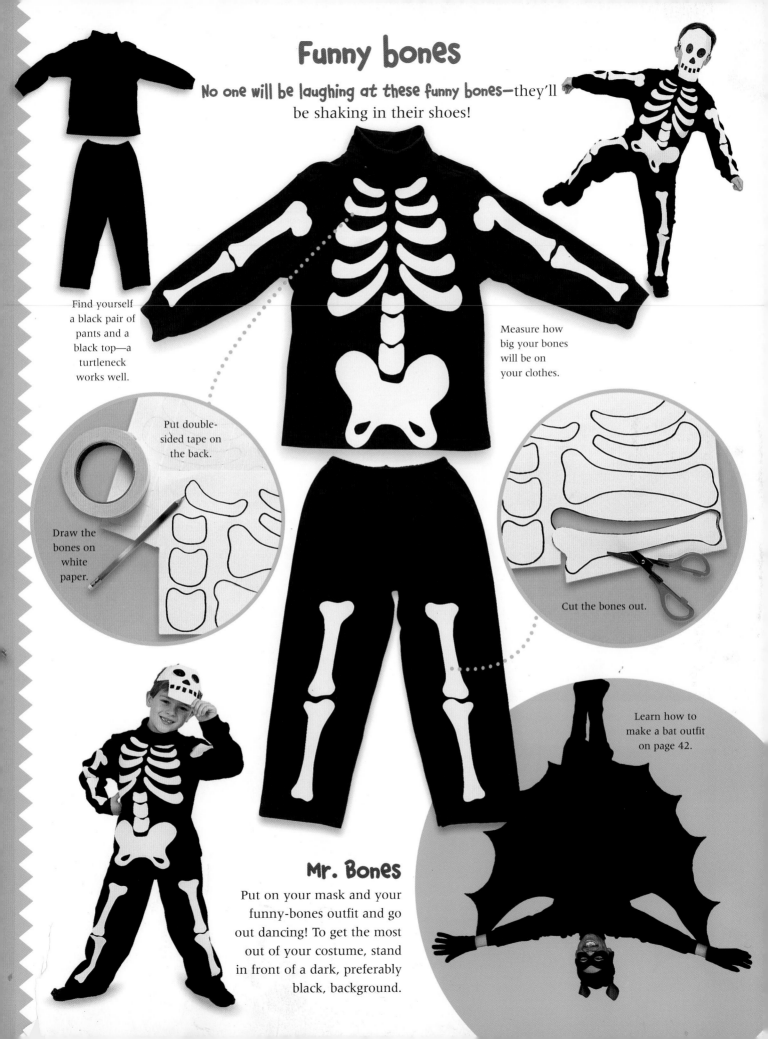

Find yourself a black pair of pants and a black top—a turtleneck works well.

Measure how big your bones will be on your clothes.

Put double-sided tape on the back.

Draw the bones on white paper.

Cut the bones out.

Learn how to make a bat outfit on page 42.

Mr. Bones

Put on your mask and your funny-bones outfit and go out dancing! To get the most out of your costume, stand in front of a dark, preferably black, background.

Bat cape

Glove

Glove

Create your cape

You need a piece of black fabric for your cape. To measure how much, hold the fabric with outstretched arms and that will be your widest edge. Fold it in half to cut it.

Attach the gloves to the material with a safety pin.

You will need:

Black fabric
Gloves
Hat and mask
Safety pins
Pen or chalk for marking fabric
Scissors/pinking shears

Cut the fabric

Take a square piece of fabric and fold it in half.

Draw the cape pattern with chalk, making sure the fold is on the left side.

Cut the fabric with pinking shears or carefully with scissors.

Bat hat

Mask

Cut a mask shape out of cardboard, poke a hole in each side, and thread a piece of string through.

Bat ears

It's just a wool hat with some paper ears.

Cut two ear shapes out of black paper.

Pin the ears to the hat with a safety pin.

Pin the center of the cape to your top with a safety pin.

All you need for your bat outfit is a black top, black leggings, and black shoes.

Fairy cape

Create your cape

As with the bat cape, find a large piece of pink material and hold it out with your arms outstretched. This will be the width of your cape. Cut it into a large rectangle and fold the material in half.

Tie each end of the cape onto a bracelet.

Cut it out

Fold the fabric in half and draw on the pattern as shown, making sure the fold is on the left side.

Cut the fabric out with scissors or pinking shears.

Use safety pins to attach the cape to your T-shirt.

wings for things

Everyone needs wings at some point in life. And they are so simple to make.

Angel

Impish bat

wing shape

Choose the shape that you would like your wings to be—soft lines for the fairy or angel wings, or pointed for the impish ones. You will need thick cardboard to make the wings—try a large cardboard box.

Fold a piece of paper in half and draw the shape of your wing on it.

......Fold

Unfold the paper and lay it on a big piece of thick cardboard. Draw around it.

Ask an adult:
to help you cut out the wing shape.

Lay the shape on construction paper, draw around it, and cut it out.

Glue the paper onto the wings.

Glitter and sparkle

Now for the fun part! It's time to add a bit of a shine to your wings. You could sprinkle some glitter onto them or decorate them with pieces of construction paper—cut up magazines work well too.

·· Make four holes using the tip of a pen.

Ask an adult:
to help you make the holes.

Back view

··Thread two pieces of elastic through the holes as straps.

Front view

···Cut out colored paper and glue it on.

Use craft glue (see page 47). ······

Add glitter

Glue a pattern on your wings, then sprinkle on the glitter. When you have covered the glue, shake it off onto a sheet of newspaper.

No-sew dressing up

All the outfits in just need some handy

Smart scissors

Pinking shears mean no hemming.

Velcro
Velcro is a great way to attach clothing. Make sure you buy the Velcro with the adhesive back.

Pinking shears
Cut the edge of your outfit with these scissors to stop the material from fraying.

Ask an adult
When you read this, always ask an adult to help you.

this book can be made without sewing machines or hand sewing. You may safety pins and Velcro. Pinking shears are also useful for a "no fray" edge.

Staplers

Costumes are often worn only a few times, so a stapler can be used instead of sewing. They are particularly useful when working with fabric and cardboard together.

Safety pins

Safety pins are the most useful when you are attaching fabric to fabric, for example, attaching the fairy cape to a T-shirt.

Buy them in bunches.

Tapes and glues

It is essential that you are equipped with tape and glue when you are making costumes. Make sure you have them on hand before you start.

Packing tape

Thick packing tape is useful when working with cardboard boxes.

Thin tape

Thin tape is better for smaller accessories.

Double-sided tape

Double-sided tape is a clean way of attaching paper and cardboard, and it's strong too.

Glue stick

Glue stick is great for sticking paper to paper...

Craft glue

... but craft glue is stronger and is better when working with cardboard AND covering with glitter.

Ask an adult: it's always worth asking an adult to help you glue things.

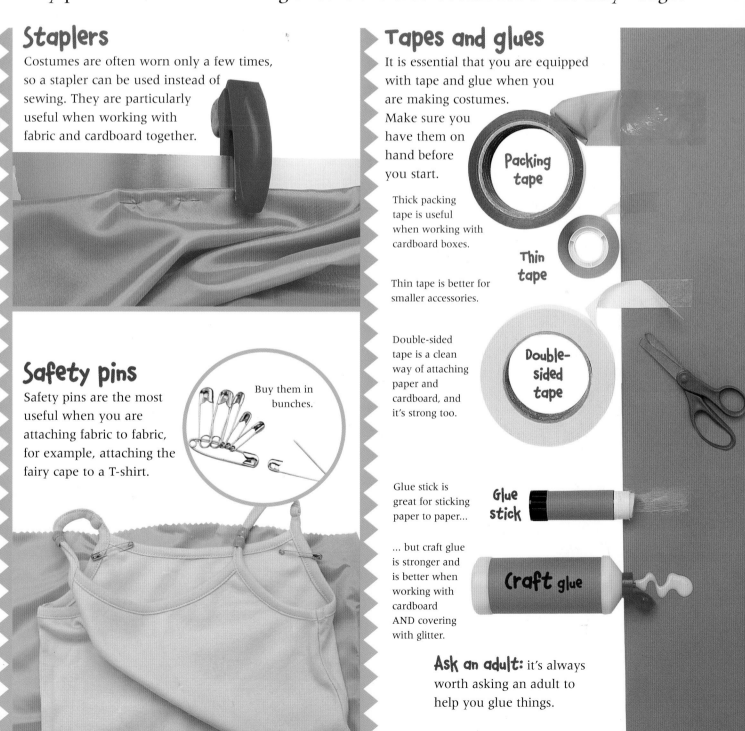

Microphone

A handy prop for reporters, pop stars, and important news. As seen on page 12.

You will need:

A ball
A cardboard tube
Kitchen foil
Black paper
Sticky tape
Cord or string

Tape the ball to the top of the tube.

Wrap the foil around the ball and tape it down.

Wrap some black paper around the tube.

Tape the paper in place.

Tape the end of the cord to the inside of the tube.

Index

Acknowledgments

With thanks to:
Thomas Arlon, James Bull, Jordan Clarkson, Eleanor Coldwell, Evie Coldwell, Renae Dawes, Olivia Hurdle, Daniel Olorunfemi, and Louis Stride
for being model heroes.

All images © Dorling Kindersley.
For further information see: www.dkimages.com